Our Land
OUR SOUL

Majestic Teton Valley—
The Teton's Western Slope

ERIC I. SOYLAND

The canyons of the Teton River (pictured right) with her brother and sister river/canyons – Badger Creek and Bitch Creek – form one of the most dramatic eco-systems in America.

All three river/canyons are spawning grounds for the Yellowstone Cutthroat trout – a species considered to be of greatest conservation need by the state of Idaho and also a candidate species for listing under the Federal Endangered Species Act – home also are these river/canyons to virtually all species of Rocky Mountain birds and animals.

Truly unique and one of a kind these wild river/canyons – a treasure in Teton Valleys midst and indeed a national treasure.

Let them exist untouched – let us and future generations enjoy and cherish their grandeur.

Let them always be as the Creator intended – wild, natural and free for eternity without human interference.

ISBN 10: 1-59152-081-9
ISBN 13: 978-1-59152-081-8

© 2011 by Eric I. Soyland

Edited by Eric I. Soyland and Eric Dingemanse
Written by Eric I. Soyland
Photographs by Eric I. Soyland
Introduction by Eric I. Soyland
Published by LATITUDE 56° SOUTH PUBLISHING AND PRODUCTION, LLC

You may order extra copies of this book by calling Farcountry Press toll free at (800) 821-3874.

Produced by Sweetgrass Books.

sweetgrassbooks
a division of Farcountry Press

PO Box 5630, Helena, MT 59604; (800) 821-3874; www.sweetgrassbooks.com.

Printed in China.

15   14   13   12   11   1   2   3   4   5

The canyons of the Teton River—a treasure in Teton Valley's midst, and indeed a national treasure.

Let these river canyons exist untouched for eternity— let us and future generations enjoy and cherish their beauty, their wildlife, their grandeur.

Dedication

*This book is dedicated to all of us who love this
oh so magic land, Teton Valley, as I do.*

*And to all the organizations working so diligently to insure
she remains one of the worlds pristine places
– Teton Regional Land Trust, Vard, Friends of the Teton river,
Trout Unlimited and so many others.*

*And, oh yes, Earthfire Institute; you all work so hard and are
appreciated not only by me and many, many others, but by the land
herself – her rivers, canyons, mountains, animals and forests and
I am sure by all the human inhabitants that come to know her.*

Thank you so, so much for your efforts.

*Please enjoy this book – indeed it is a culmination
of my deep love and respect for this valley.*

For those who love her, Teton Valley, truly is our land, our soul.

From a wagonmasters' diary
—1887 or thereabouts.
The settling of Teton Valley,
Idaho and Wyoming.

Long and hard, that journey to
paradise, so long, long ago and
yet, and yet, faith and a heartfelt
knowing drove them on.

Up through Utah territory, the
wagon trains came – North to
Idaho, then East out of Rexburg.

So many wagons, so many men, women, children, dogs and horses – some with a cow even – carrying dreams and hopes on a wagon, day after day, after dusty day.

Go East out of
Rexburg, the stories
said. Look for a snow
white peak reaching
out for and caressing
a blue, oh so blue, sky.

*A peak so imposing, so Grand as to dominate
the sky itself and, yes, surrounding that
grand mountain will be three others of lesser
size, brothers of the Grand one and there,
at their feet, will be spread the tablecloth
of dreams and hopes come true.*

One Afternoon

Skies of mist
Skies of snow
A strong wind runs
And snow squalls,
Majestic white curtains dot my horizon.
And as I hike amidst this wild beauty
A glance up shows me a hawk,
His silhouette so plain against the moving wall of snow
And as I watch he plays
Thousands of feet above my canyon rim,
Vertically now, straight up toward the sky he flies on extended wings
And then folding those wings plummets straight down – now not a
Hawk but a stone –
toward the canyon floor.
And as I watch, the wings so quickly extend breaking his fall –
Now accelerating with just a single thrust,
A single beat of powerful wings,
Again vertically up towards a waiting sky.
I watch amazed
And yes, again at the very steepest part of flight
The apex of his climb –
Wings fold and the free fall begins.
Before a bird, now a stone.
How long I watched,
So many minutes transfixed.
Snow moving fast on the wind,
The hawk so obvious at play.
And time and time again
Against the magnificent curtain of snow,
Mountain canyon and river.
He played a game of life
A game of death.
So simply a celebration – both of flight,
Of freedom and life.
And I allowed to watch
And then continue my own journey
A happier more fulfilled man.

Go to it – start a new life in
a paradise so pristine, so
pure as to be most assuredly
created from above.

And yes, oh my yes,
the stories proved true,
a thousand times over!

"Whoa," I yelled, the command echoing from wagon to wagon,
horse to horse, man to man – the great train of wagons slowed
then halted and, oh my, yes, people spilled onto the ground
all gathering together looking East.

And there to the East the Grand Mountain of stories reflected towards us a dazzling path of welcoming light – a path of so white light to guide us the rest of our way home.

Tears were shed that day, I can tell you — tears of joy, tears of anticipation and now laughter and yells filling the air, for before us lay the Valley — our goal, our hope.

We looked at one another almost in disbelief – A dream I thought, oh yes
I'm dreaming but no for we all saw the same, we all felt solid ground
beneath our feet, we all felt the restlessness, the need in our hearts.
No, certainly, not a dream – real it was!!

Guarded by those magic mountains lay a valley of pristine rivers, meadows,
timber and canyons, yes animals galore. What more could be asked of the
Eternal Light, for all our needs and dreams have been met and more!

Hours passed as we played, made plans, hugged and cried but finally my
words – "Onword, our home awaits, Giddiup!" – rang out for all to hear and
obey and with my arm signal to proceed, we began the descent to paradise.
My yes, oh my yes, we found our earthly paradise.

Years pass, oh my they do, so quickly — towns were born, the valley grew
with names like Judkins, Tetonia, Driggs, Victor and Alta.

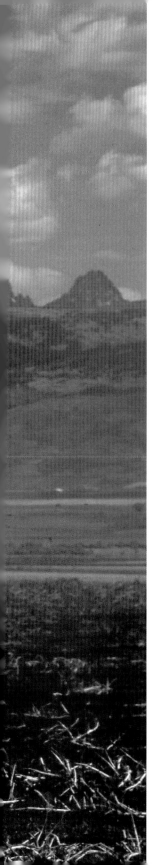

The land fertile enough for we were not greedy folk – winters long!
Yes, and often hard but the land gave enough and always those
mountains to our East warmed our hearts and caressed
our souls on even the coldest of nights.

A fierce love we had for this land – its rivers, meadows, canyons and mountains. But an even greater love we had for the animals, for they became our friends.

Special gifts from above were those animals.
For they were here before us and like us had families, friends, needs and
emotions; we were the interlopers, the trespassers on their land.

Is it not right; is it not fair to show respect, compassion and love
for a land and its creatures that welcomes us?
Is this not, we asked ourselves, our universal responsibility?

Good stewards and guardians we strived to become, for both this pristine land and its animal inhabitants, for they gave us their hearts, their souls, their land.

*And now I, the wagonmaster – my name is not important to this tale – having allowed the
reading of my personal diary from so many years ago needs to continue this visit in the present
time, for I have been, since my passing from this earth 100 or so years ago, far away
in the service of the Eternal Light and only now have a moment to pay attention
to the Valley which cradles my heart and my soul.*

You understand now people of the 21st Century how we found this land. I can only call it the greatest gift from above and yes it was, and yes it will always be.

*But sadly came
the day of my
passing and with
my passing another
calling, equally if
not more important
– my earth body
passed but my soul
and spirit lived
on and flew, in
the service of the
Eternal Light.*

Busy I've been – the Valley still in my heart, after almost 100 years away, but now today I look down once more on this so precious land, a land still so dominant in my soul. Oh, to see you again, my precious Valley and what you have become.

Memories, now flooding over me – should I speak? Yes!, for I have been chosen, I am the voice of the Eternal Light, my tongue cannot be held. Tears now blurring my vision – cry I do and cry I will for I do not understand what I see before me. How to understand, I ask myself, the loss of so many farms. Such precious land now cut up willy-nilly into tiny squares. Most inhabited only by weeds where once was grain waving in a warm summer wind.

How to understand our glass clear rivers of old, now polluted.
How to understand our so precious animal friends – the elk, deer, bears, moose,
wolves, coyotes and others now afraid for their lives and understandably for
they are hunted not simply for much needed food but also sport and yes, their
annual migration trails of centuries past blocked by houses and roads.

Yes, cry I did, cry I do and cry I will for such a loss!!
How to understand in so few years of my absence that God's own home,
a valley so pristine, truly one of a kind on earth and blessed
in every way can be torn and changed.

What has become of the words we lived by – caring, compassion, respect, love, live and let live for our animal neighbors, and the responsibility of being good stewards of the land, for the land is not ours, it belongs to the planet Earth and we for a short while are its caretakers.

Is the need for more and more dollars, more and more material things,
so strong in the hearts of men that our future is being sold?

A Violent Spring Storm, March 31st, Evening – The Tetons

We walk, Free and I, on this wild night.
As we always walk – a nightly walk, to salute a setting sun.
And, so suddenly I see April.
Dusk comes, a tired sun, now retreating, low in the western sky.
Covered by evening clouds, wild angry clouds, a fierce wind.

"Free, look, I see April, look Free, across our canyon river."
She rides, April does, atop all white horses of swirling snow
– pushed hard by this angry, so powerful, relentless wind.
A swirling wind, a spring wind, helping April.
April comes, she comes, "Free look" and she waves.
High and strong she rides the wind, the wind her friend, pushing April.
A wind much stronger than I ever recall – clouds of snow billowing high, following April.

A dust storm of snow helping April, protecting April.
April now ahead. Turning, smiling, looking our way.

A nod as if to say, I am April.
We'll meet tomorrow, my first day, when the storm has set me free.

I am April

*NO, to those that fail to place above all other considerations,
the conservation and protection of our waters, our forests,
our mountain views, our rolling fields and most importantly
the safety and welfare of our wild animal friends.*

But say yes, yes, yes, in loud voices to him or her that presents a solid plan based on caring and love – profit yes, nothing is wrong with a reasonable profit, for men and their families need to live but this oh so precious land, Teton Valley and its creatures, need also to live and they have been here for millenniums and will outlast the brief footprints made by man.

For once despoiled, the land can never again return to what it was for the hands of a clock turn only forward, never back.

*This land, oh beautiful land, now
cries as I do, for I hear its voice,
feel its wet, wet tears touch
and run down my face.*

I beseech you, all who love this Valley, in the name of the Eternal Light – open your eyes!
Act quickly! Yes, more so for you Mr. and Mrs. Elected ones – those who hold high the staff
of power – for life on the planet is often short and time seems to pass all of us by too swiftly.
The time to act is now!

A shawl woven of love and respect
for the land and all living creatures
must be cast over this so special
Valley for the land itself will
exist into eternity but its health,
wellbeing and beauty as well
as the wellbeing of its creatures
depends solely on thoughtful
planning, caring, compassion,
respect and love.

*I have watched and learned –
something called a Land Trust
exists in the 21st Century. Learn
about them, work together and
for eternity our so precious
land and its' inhabitants will be
protected and continue to share
life and beauty as partners with
generations to follow.*

Now I must leave you for the Eternal Light calls me home but return one day I will for this wonderful Valley will always, into eternity, warm my heart for indeed it is and will always be – our land, our soul.

A heavy heart have I but also, yes, a strong knowingness that righteousness will prevail.

Walk with lighter steps – I do – for my words must be heeded.

Each animal has a legend behind it.
Each plant has a spirit within it.
We bring upon ourselves injustice,
if we are not in harmony with respect
to each living matter that God has created.

—Travis Parashonts of the Cedar Band of Paiutes

Time is not on your side – ACT!

The Eternal Light commanded my speech to you, oh Valley people, and I the wagonmaster of so many years ago, has honored the wish for I have learned that the only path is the path leading to truth, honesty, compassion, empathy and caring, directed not only at man but embracing also the land and all living creatures – for all who inhabit this world are equal in his eyes. That is his wish, that is his command and that is the path towards the Light!

I remind you again, – listen to my words! Walk the path of the light – turn your backs
and your souls away from the darkness, for light is the path and the path is the light.
We will visit again, people of Teton Valley, for my love of this Valley knows
no bounds, flowing like blood through my body, my heart, my soul.

Until then, — oh, oh,
but wait, forgive me for
I am old and my memory
suffers – two gifts I have to
make your journey easier
– both more priceless than
gold – my friends
Mr. Wisdom and
Mr. Hope.

*Mister Wisdom makes hard choices easier for he is the light shining
bright along a difficult to walk path and yes for you, Teton Valley,
hard choices lay ahead – certainly we all can use a talk
with Mr. Wisdom now and again – can't we?*

Use Mr. Wisdom, then speak also to your own heart for the truth is always buried there – we just have to find it and listen – and realize your decisions of today are chiseled in stone for generations to come – many will be unpopular now but oh so necessary for the eternal wellbeing of this land and its creatures.

Oh, yes, don't let me leave and forget my friend Mr. Hope – such an important gift!
For Hope is the match that lights the fire of miracles!

Always, always allow hope into your heart and soul –
miracles will follow, and we all have need for miracles.

Again I sense the Eternal Light calling.
Tarry I must no longer.

If I'm needed simply speak to me from your heart,
answer I will during your dreamstate.
And yes, Teton Valley, you have the strength and
the wisdom to proceed, DO IT!!
And as for me, the wagonmaster, I count
the moments till I return.